Will Kirk
restore

Will Kirk
restore

The art of caring for
the things you love

CONTENTS

INTRO

DUCTION

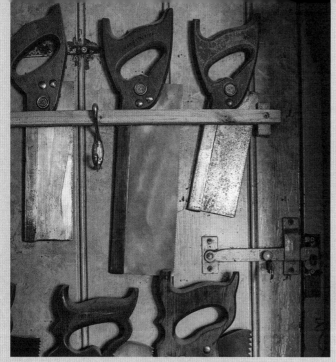

Restore (verb):

To return something to an earlier condition, or to bring something back into existence.

When something comes into my workshop or the BBC's *The Repair Shop,* I have no idea where it has been, who has loved it and the stories it has seen. All tangible items have a history. Each mark, dent or knock is there because it has been used by someone and has been part of a family or place, and that is all part of its charm. Whether it is a dining table where relationships have been formed and stories told or a mahogany writing desk where careers have been forged and deals done, it will tell its own unique story. I will never strip a piece of furniture back completely because that history is all part of its character. A piece of furniture can connect our present to the past and, once restored, to the future.

Each item I work on will be unique, and old furniture is incredibly well made so that it can be cleaned and restored to last another few decades or even add a hundred years to its life. We live in a world where the circular mentality has been replaced by the desire for convenience and trend-led fast interiors. Give it a few years, and many of these factory-made and cheap items will be in a landfill. Older items are inherently more valuable, and virtually any wooden piece can be restored; in my experience, the older the piece, the more repairable it is.

I think, as humans, we are hardwired to enjoy the tactile quality of wood and other tangible items. I love the satisfaction of seeing a piece being slowly but surely transformed. The processes of restoring furniture are also incredibly absorbing, allowing me to focus on the job at hand so I can empty my mind of other things. It can be repetitive and slow, making it a calming pursuit. Some days, when restoring a piece of furniture, I might never return home if I didn't have a wife and child! As a pastime, restoration offers a sense of escapism, and it can facilitate moments of productivity and peacefulness that can sometimes feel few and far between in our technology-driven environments.

Restoration inherently involves a lot of problem-solving. No matter how simple an item is, there is always something new to learn. Often, deciding what to do to get the best results can be a challenge, but falling upon the correct technique and executing it is so rewarding.

Whilst some of the work I do is very specialist, and I would always advise contacting an expert if you are

unsure, there is a myriad of things you can do yourself at home to restore furniture items and other treasures bringing, them back to their former glory. It is often not as big and scary as it might seem. You also do not need a lot of materials to transform a piece of furniture. With some know-how, skill and practice, anyone can have a go. A lot of restoration, such as polishing and waxing, is reversible, so if you go wrong, you can reverse a bit and have another go. Even the simplest of changes, such as cleaning a piece of furniture and adding a thin coat of polish, can give you a massive boost of confidence and encourage you to go further. I promise you do not need to be a woodworking genius with years of experience to get started.

There is something truly special about an item that has been made by hand. In this country, many crafts, trades and skills, from arrow- and copper-smithing to silk weaving and hand engraving, are dying out. The Heritage Crafts Red List documents traditional crafts by the likelihood that they will not survive to the next generation. As master craftsmen have turned to other skill sets or passed away without sharing their knowledge, we risk losing the crafts that favour patience and precision. If these skills disappear, then we significantly reduce the opportunities for future generations to establish more sustainable lifestyles and deal with future challenges.

Some skills provide a link back to our ancestors and how they lived and allow us to carry this invisible thread of knowledge forward. Restoring wooden furniture is just one of these skills.

MY STORY

I am amazed that I am doing something I love so much as my career, and looking back, it happened almost by chance. My grandfather was a furniture restorer, and I have memories of him painting a meticulous faux marble fireplace with a feather and heading off to his workshop at every opportunity. Like me, he was not a fan of school, and he was a huge inspiration. I grew up in Clapham and struggled academically. I was drawn to more practical subjects, like art, and all the girls were in the art studio, too, so it's where I spent most of my time! I loved painting and working with my hands. Woodworking wasn't seen as particularly cool or a subject that would lead to a career, so art seemed like a better route.

I was daunted by the idea of going straight to university, so I decided to do an Art Foundation course at Camberwell School of Art. It was one of the best years of my life because I felt like I had broken away from stuffy academia into creativity, where nothing was a bad idea. I was channelled into the graphic design pathway (as opposed to fine art or illustration) and gained a place on a degree course at the London College of Communication. After failing the first year, I tried to take it again, unsure whether I had been enjoying Freshers' Week too much or if I just wasn't very good at graphic design. It was the latter, and I retreated home, unsure of what the future would hold for me.

A few weeks later, I was in the garden at my mum's house when she came out with the newspaper and showed me a course advertised in the small ads in the back. It was for antique furniture restoration at London Metropolitan University. I knew nothing about it or even that such a thing existed, but it was practical and sounded interesting. I was the youngest student by about four decades, but after the first day in the workshop, I never looked back. It was hands-on, methodical and practical work, with creativity and problem-solving rolled together.

While there, I was lucky enough to represent the university with the Worshipful Company of Painters-Stainers at the annual Salon Decorative Arts Fair in Bergamo, Italy in 2012. It gave me an insight into an incredible community of so many different and skilled artisans from across the world and opened my eyes to the possibilities for my career.

After finishing my degree, I spent a year at an antique restoration company in Clapham, but after a year of sweeping up and fetching endless cups of tea for other members of staff and the offer of a five-pence pay rise, I decided to go into business on my own. My dad had passed away, and I had inherited a small sum of money, so I decided to use this to hire a workshop. I took a leap of faith and found a space where I could work, handed in my notice at my job, and set out on my own.

It was scary at the time and a glacial-paced start, to say the least. I printed out a thousand flyers and paid one of my friends to come and distribute them with me in places like Chelsea and Kensington, where I knew there would be homes stuffed with the types of furniture that needed work. It was in the depths of winter, all the post boxes were frozen shut and we couldn't prise them open because our hands were so numb. It was a pretty sobering time, and around me, my friends were launching successful careers in the City or elsewhere and seemed to be moving out into their own homes.

Slowly but surely, my marketing efforts paid off, and I started building a name for myself, mainly through word of mouth. One job for one well-connected client soon meant I was doing up pieces for all her well-heeled neighbours and friends, who owned some incredible items between them. I learnt more on the job than I did at university and made a fair few mistakes along the way. When I started, I was driving to North London to fix a chair for £20 without charging delivery, thus making a loss, but once I found the right people and was passed different items through them, I was soon at a stage where I was turning work away. I was lucky enough to restore some remarkable heirlooms and one-off pieces.

It was a chance encounter with someone from a production company who asked me to restore a bench that led me to *The Repair Shop* and then *The Travelling Auctioneers*. During the first season of *The Repair Shop*, I wondered whether people expected an old wizard with a cane to fix up furniture, so as a young person, I felt that I had a lot to prove. Pretty quickly, though, I realised my worries were unfounded, and it's fantastic being able to teach the other presenters something or ask for their help when I am stuck on a project.

The Repair Shop is such a unique programme, and it is fantastic to work with a group of people who love what they do so much. There are 600 years of experience on the show, but we are all still learning.

We have a shared passion, and that really shines through. The set, which is located at The Weald & Downland Living Museum, is idyllic and really is as peaceful as it looks. As well as the challenge of transforming the pieces that come to us, I adore looking at the face of the person who has brought it in when they see what we have done and that it looks like they remembered. It is a win-win.

How to Use This Book
—

Whether furniture restoration is a firm hobby or you have never even considered restoring something in your home, I hope this book will inspire you to have a go.

As we reconnect with a love of antique and vintage furniture, combined with more awareness of sustainability, I would love to share some of my knowledge and the creative and emotional rewards that restoring furniture brings.

I will first guide you through the basics, including how to set up a workshop, identify different woods, spot a gem and look after furniture before and after any restoration work. I will then look at quick fixes, like removing watermarks, scratches, blisters and dents, and cleaning wood.

In the next chapter, I will demystify types of finishing, including waxing, polishing, stains, pigments and oiling. The speed at which you progress through the book is entirely up to you. Maybe you have an old table or item that would be a good starting point? If you are a beginner, I recommend reading from the beginning in order to try out some of the techniques.

In the second half of the book, I will tackle some larger projects, including restoring a chair, sideboard and table. This will incorporate some of the techniques covered earlier in the book, plus some new ones.

The final chapter will include details of my essential tools, a tool index and recommended brushes.

Above all, enjoy the process and take as long as you need to hone your techniques.

Happy restoring!

Love Will x

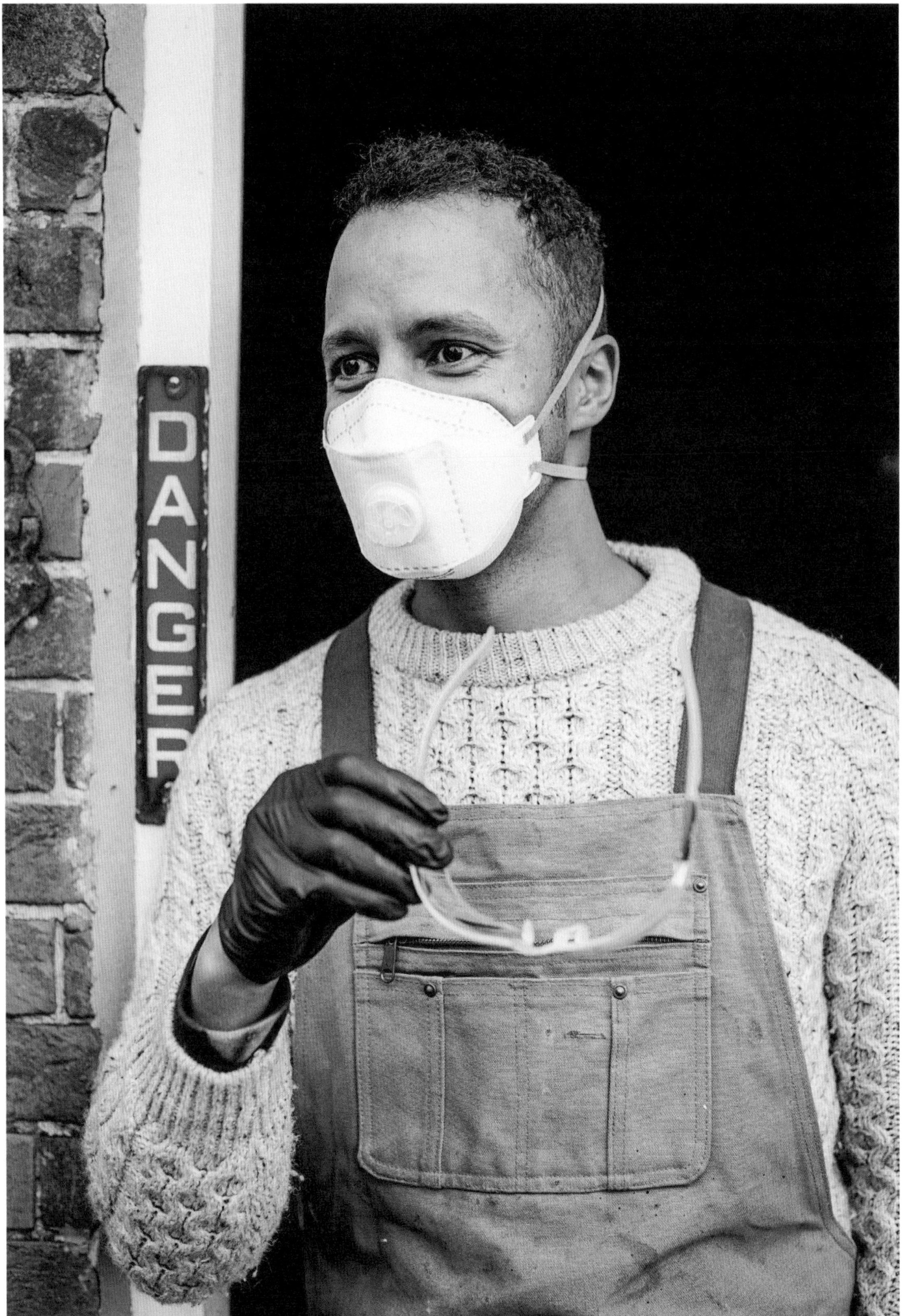
DANGER

NOTES ON SAFETY

There are many things to consider when working with wood and tools, particularly if you are working on your own, but here are just a few of my tips.

Wear the right clothing

- Whenever you buy a new tool or piece of machinery, always read through the instructions and work out which protective clothing is appropriate, in order to stay safe whilst using it.
- Eye protection is a must, as is a mask for sanding. Always ensure you wear safety glasses or goggles, as small bits of wood and dust often fly around and can cause long-term damage without the right eyewear. There are different options available, including goggles that fit over glasses, so choose something comfortable so you can almost forget you are wearing them!
- There are different masks, depending on the work, but there are general models that will help protect your lungs by filtering out dust particles and will seal snugly to your face. I also use gloves to protect my hands when working with raw wood, French polish, solvents or other chemicals.
- Heavy-duty and closed-toe footwear, such as steel-capped boots, will stop you from breaking a toe if you accidentally drop something. I also wear an apron so my clothes do not get mucky, and it has pockets in the front so I can carry my tape measure and pencil with me as I move around the workshop. Avoid loose or baggy clothing that could get snagged or tangled in your equipment, and tie long hair back.

Keep your space clean and tidy

- Airflow in your workshop is really important, so keep any windows open. If I am stripping back any type of wood or spray-painting furniture, I always go outside to do the job. My sander has an inbuilt dust extractor that limits the mess in my workshop, and many products have this feature. If you are finishing furniture, you do not want sawdust in the air because it will stick, so it's important to keep the environment clean and always advisable to do this work outside if you can.

● Do not leave items lying around; make sure your floor space is free from obstacles and trip hazards. I use an off-cuts bin to store bits of unused wood for future projects. Also, ensure you have enough light to see exactly what you are doing.

Stay focused

● Whether it's a hobby or you are taking it more seriously, operating machinery and woodworking tools can be very dangerous. I'll always let someone know if I am using electric saws so they don't come up behind me and give me a surprise, for example. Even if you are at home, doing some sanding, it pays to let your family or people you live with know what you are doing – and don't let the kids anywhere near your workspace! Keep your mobile phone in another location entirely or switched off.

● If you are tired, take regular breaks because it can be easy to lose focus or concentration.

Keep tools and bits sharp

● Always read all instructions for any new equipment before you get started because it is easy to underestimate their capability or power or misjudge what they are suitable for – do not learn the hard way. As well as this, it is important to keep woodworking tools sharp. Like kitchen knives, the sharper they are, the better they will work. A sharp blade will make it safer to use by reducing the likelihood of kickback and will ensure the cleanest cut possible.

● If you plan on doing a lot of woodworking, investing in high-quality pieces made from more durable materials that will not need to be sharpened as often makes sense.

WHEN SHOULD YOU
GO TO AN EXPERT?

Sometimes, it can be hard to know when to seek advice, and this is always a bit of a grey area, with no right or wrongs. On *The Repair Shop*, I will have a go at repairing or restoring any type of item, but there are times when, if it is not my specialist area, such as metal-working, I will ask one of the others if I am unsure. With the tips and tricks in this book, I hope you will be confident to tackle most basic things. However, if an item is very valuable, sentimental or irreplaceable, I would talk to an expert.

The British Antique Furniture Restorers' Association (BAFRA) is an organisation of qualified people in furniture conservation, restoration and repair, and you can search on their website (www.bafra.org.uk) for local experts in your area. They will be able to offer you advice about the best next steps.

'BEAUTIFUL OLD FURNITURE
HAS BEEN MADE TO LAST, SO
TRYING TO REPAIR IT WHEN
IT IS DAMAGED MAKES SENSE'

THE BASICS

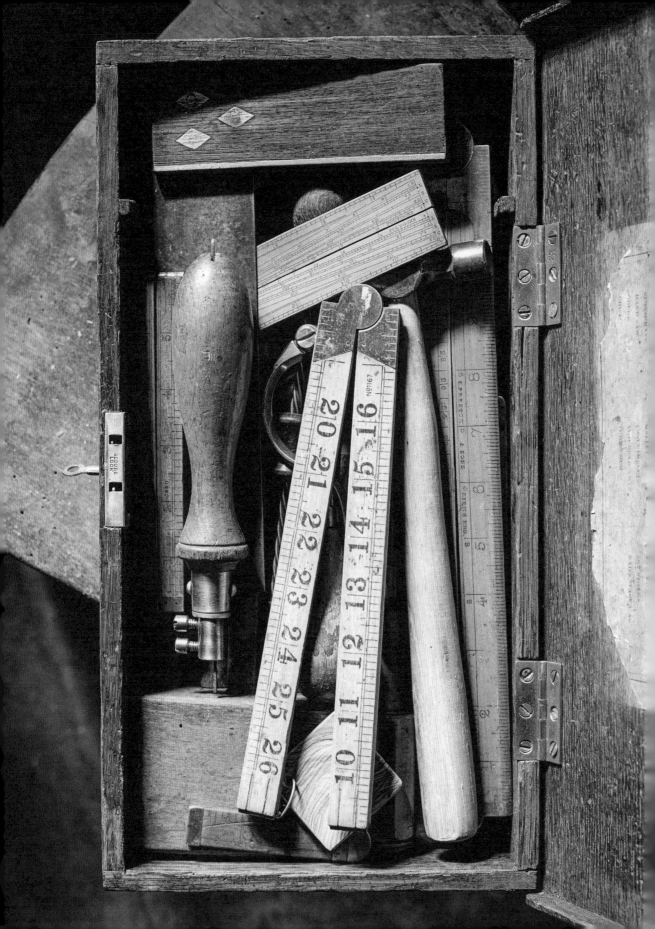

SETTING UP
YOUR WORKSHOP

The first part of setting up any type of woodworking workshop
is thinking about how much space you have. It could be any part
of your home – such as a basement, garage or shed – and you do
not need loads of room to get started. You'll need some storage,
lighting and power; ideally, it will be somewhere that you can
have some peace and quiet to completely focus on the task at hand.

Your workbench

Every good workshop starts with a workbench. It needs to be the
right height for whatever you are working with. Different projects
will require varying amounts of workbench space. I use a traditional
wooden workbench with a vice and compartments for my tools on
the side, but it was expensive, so it depends on what you plan to do.

A folding workbench or a trestle table with plywood balanced on
top can be ideal because the plywood size can be changed depending
on the item you are restoring. A folding workbench can also be raised
by putting wooden blocks underneath and easily stashed away to free
up more space when it is not in use. These can be bought relatively
inexpensively from hardware shops. It also means that if you have
outdoor space and are sanding and stripping furniture or spraying
it, you can move it outside quite easily.

Lighting

Lighting is critical, not only so you can see what you are doing
clearly but also so the intricate work is more straightforward. The
best type of lighting emulates normal daylight. These lightbulbs can
be quite blue in normal living spaces but will give an accurate colour
reproduction of natural light. It is also ideal if the walls are white
to reflect or maximise the light.

Not long ago, I was repairing some cracks and splits in the wood at the top of an old grandfather clock. I used my stains to colour-match the wood and was delighted with the result. When I took it outside to show it to someone, it looked awful. The light inside had been too warm. I won't make that mistake again!

Storage

Good storage is another must-have, so your tools are protected from the environment. Unfortunately, it's hard to stop tools from rusting. I regularly clean and oil my tools to protect them from moisture in the environment, but at *The Repair Shop*, everything is getting a bit rusty as my tools are exposed.

I tend to hang my regular tools so they are easily accessible. This is a great way to use wall and ceiling space in a workshop, which might otherwise be redundant. If you know you are not returning to your workshop for a few days, I advise storing all tools in hard-wearing storage boxes. Keep groups of tools together in a neat fashion, ready for use.

Drawers can also be useful for marking and measuring tools, nails, hardware and other bits and pieces. If I make something up, like a cleaner or French polish, I will always label it with what it is and the date I made it, so I know what I am dealing with and when it is likely to need replacing.

You will also need a home for all flammable liquids and solvents, and if you are working a lot with flammables, you can buy special fireproof cabinets so they can safely be stored in one place.

In terms of covering items I am working on so they don't get knocked or damaged, I wait until they are completely dry and cover them in wool furniture removal blankets, which are very cheap.

OAK 6x6"
BLANKS
£8·00
each

IDENTIFYING
TYPES OF WOOD

When restoring old wooden furniture, it is crucial to identify the species of wood you are working with because this can help you select the appropriate finish or stain. All woods absorb the finish in unique ways and different types of wood require varying kinds of finishes so they look good and are protected. There are many, many types of wood, and they are identifiable from their colour, grain, texture and weight.

Woods are divided into hardwoods and softwoods. Hardwoods come from deciduous trees and are dense and of higher quality. Common hardwoods are oak, maple, mahogany, cherry, walnut, poplar and rubberwood. Hardwoods are often darker and more expensive than other types of wood.

Pine, spruce, redwood, hemlock, larch and cedar are examples of softwoods. These come from coniferous trees that grow more quickly and are known for their versatility. Visually, they are paler than hardwoods. Hard and softwoods are used to make furniture, but softwoods have a less dense internal structure, so tend to be lighter.

The other type of wood is manufactured wood, also called engineered wood. These woods are made by heating, bonding and compressing wood chips and sawdust, so the finished product looks like wood. Examples of this type of wood include MDF and laminated wood.

It is also important to identify if your item is veneered. Many furniture items are veneered (they have been doing it since Egyptian times!), where a very thin slice of valuable wood covers a thicker core of a less precious material, making it look like a solid piece of wood. This was done for aesthetic appeal and to make it more cost-effective. Thin veneers allow precious wood to be stretched further.

WILL'S TIP

Ensure you are working with natural wood. Veneer is different from laminate, which is a layer of plastic made to look like wood. This is much more common in fast furniture because it is cheap and factory-made.

WHAT TYPE OF WOOD IS IT?

What is the colour of the wood?
—

The colour of the wood is the surface colour and shows how it has reacted to many years of natural light exposure and natural ageing. The patina describes how the wood looks after years of polishing, rubbing and dusting, alongside oxidation of the polished surface and exposure to the sun. All materials will develop a patina over time, and wood patination can give you some insights into the age of an item of furniture. For example, older furniture may have a richer and deeper patina compared with newer pieces.

What does it look like at the end?
—

Distinguishing between natural hardwoods, softwoods and manufactured woods can be quite challenging because furniture items are made from multiple pieces of wood and some from manufactured wood. The way to tell is to look at the end or edge. If you can see the wood grain, it is solid wood. If you notice the presence of small woodchips pressed together or an inconsistency in the finish compared to the rest of the piece, the item is likely made from MDF materials. Natural woods will have unique and natural lines.

Is it veneered?
—

Furniture with chips to the surface is typical of veneer damage. Veneered furniture will have a visible edge banding or thin strip of wood around the edges and, as with solid wood, you would see the natural end grain. Often, the veneer will be discontinued at the back of the item, or you can tell by the angle of the grain and glue lines where seams are joined. Veneered furniture will also have thinner surfaces when compared to solid wood items.

Does it have unique patterns?

Veneered furniture tends to look more uniform with neatly finished patterns, whilst solid wood tends to have character with knots and a noticeable grain. Grain patterns are formed by the alignment of wood fibres, which vary among wood species. Woods like maple and birch have uniform and straight patterns, whilst oak and ash exhibit a more pronounced grain pattern with distinctive lines and texture.

With natural woods, when you run your hand over the furniture, you may even be able to feel the grain. Woods like ash and oak have a rougher texture.

Are there dovetails?

Pull out any drawers and look at where the front meets the side. If you can see an interlocking joint in the shape in the shape of little doves' tails (the clue's in the name) – it is likely solid wood. Dovetail joints are a sign of quality craftsmanship in furniture-making.

If there are no drawers, look at the corners and edges. If these feature screws or dowels, those construction methods suggest solid wood.

'ALL TANGIBLE ITEMS HAVE A HISTORY. EACH MARK, DENT OR KNOCK IS THERE BECAUSE IT HAS BEEN USED BY SOMEONE AND HAS BEEN PART OF A FAMILY OR PLACE, AND THAT IS ALL PART OF ITS CHARM'

WHERE SHOULD YOU LOOK FOR FURNITURE?

All old furniture was made to last, and I believe you pay for what you get. Older furniture will always have better components, like hinges and screws, and it can be transformed to be almost as good as new.

Buying from antique shops will always command a premium so they can cover their overheads. Many antique and flea markets sell excellent old furniture. I used to go to one at Kempton Park Racecourse where there is a bi-monthly market on a Tuesday, and from half past six in the morning there would be lots of individuals milling around, from people sourcing items for films and TV to restorers looking to snag a one-off item.

These places are generally huge, so it's a good idea to arrive with a clear sense of what you are looking for and to be early to get the best pieces. Ensure that if you need something of a specific size, like a sideboard, desk or chest of drawers to fit an alcove, for example, you have the measurements to hand. Take cash and be prepared to haggle – it's not very British, but everybody does it!

There are also local selling sites on Facebook Marketplace, eBay and Gumtree that are always worth scouring for gems, though sometimes it can be hard to see exactly what you are buying. Ideally, you should search locally so you can see your purchase before you part with your money.

HOW DO YOU SPOT A GEM?

Looking for good items is half the fun when it comes to restoration. Adding older items to your home will introduce depth and character and create a layered and interesting look. Items like sideboards are ideal because they look great but can double up as storage. Due to their shape, they also fit quite easily into modern homes. Many of us are living in smaller and smaller new-build homes, and a lot of the traditional furniture that I repair was made a long time ago and designed for larger properties. Lots of my friends have inherited items, but they are so huge that they have had to send them for auction. My flat is slim and long, so I have to think quite carefully about what I buy so it tucks away neatly.

A gem is an item that not only fits into your home but is versatile and small enough that you won't stub your toe on it and you can take it with you if you move to another property. Make sure you take your measurements carefully before purchasing.

Always look for solid wood because it is easier to finish and restore. Familiarise yourself with the different wood types used to make furniture during different periods so you can determine whether it is worth the price. There are no rights or wrongs when it comes to older items. I love Georgian furniture because it is well-designed, practical furniture with incredible attention to detail and exceptional craftsmanship that you do not find today. It is often made from mahogany and oak, which are wonderful woods to work with. I adore the clean and elegant shapes, like the sabre legs that flare into a concave formation. My mum has four Georgian chests of drawers that are still kicking around – and look fantastic – after hundreds of years.

Try not to be scared of really old items – the scratches and wear and tear during their past life are all part of their appeal. Even though I live in a modern apartment, I still have some Georgian chairs. I think many people believe that old and antique furniture is something you find at your gran's house. This is not true; those pieces can lend themselves to modern surroundings and homes. In my opinion, white walls and modern fittings with the odd old item of furniture can look great and Georgian pieces can really lend themselves to this. A house should contain a collection of things that you love, and that feel meaningful, and the odd heirloom or piece of old furniture can offer a great aesthetic in even the most contemporary space.

CLEANING YOUR NEW FIND

Before I get stuck into restoring any furniture, I usually start by thoroughly cleaning the woodwork. Removing dirt or grime before getting started allows me to see more clearly what I am working with and can reveal any further hidden areas of damage.

Learning to clean wooden furniture is essential if you want your favourite items to last. Through everyday use, most furniture will become dirty from touch, dust and anything in the air, like cooking residues, resting on it, leaving the wood not looking its best.

Many people think that disinfectant or furniture cleaner is a good option. However, if you have a wooden item with polish and wax on it, the cleaner will start to melt through the surfaces, including the dirt, and then the polish. At first it will look good, but after some time cleaning your furniture this way, all the finishes will be removed, and you will be left with bare and dry wood. The key to proper wood cleaning is to remove dirt and grime without removing the finish.

'I LOVE THE SATISFACTION OF SEEING A PIECE BEING SLOWLY BUT SURELY TRANSFORMED'

Cleaning furniture with my furniture cleaner

You can buy furniture cleaner, but making your own is cheaper and more fun. I use my own wooden furniture cleaner that can be used on all waxes and finishes, including French polish, which is a shellac finish and typically harder to clean.

Many restorers use different cleaners for different types of wood, but mine is universal. My mixture contains both white spirit and methylated spirits. White spirit is a clear solvent that is great for many woodwork and DIY tasks, whilst methylated spirits is ethanol or pure alcohol and often coloured purple. Sometimes when furniture has been over-waxed, it can leave a sticky layer of excess wax on top that is tacky and will collect dust, and white spirit will melt this away. The same effect applies to French polish and methylated spirits.

My cleaner also contains linseed oil, which strengthens and protects the wood. The oil also keeps your rag lubricated and stops it from sticking to the surface.

What you need

- Linseed oil
- White spirit
- Methylated spirits
- Glass jar
- Measuring cup

How to make up the cleaner

1. Mix one part linseed oil to three parts white spirit and three parts methylated spirits.

2. Put the lid on your jar and shake into an emulsion for about 30 seconds, a bit like making a cocktail. It will have a white, creamy consistency, but as you use it, the different parts will separate quite quickly, so ensure you regularly shake it.

WILL'S TIP

If you are cleaning antique furniture with this cleaner, check the colour of your rag as you are cleaning. If it is dark brown, this is dirt from the surface. If it starts to look lighter brown – the same colour as furniture polish – you are pressing too hard and overcleaning.

What you need

- Furniture cleaner
  (see previous page)
- Clean, soft cotton rag
- Toothbrush (for legs
  and joints)
- Ultra-fine steel wool wire

How to clean your furniture

1. Make sure you are in a well-ventilated area, and always wear gloves.

2. Start by dusting the surface with a clean rag to remove any dust.

3. Test a small amount of your cleaner first on the underside of your furniture to ensure it is the right consistency.

4. Apply a generous amount of cleaner to your rag. Wipe the furniture in the direction of the grain in circular motions, paying attention to any very tacky or dirty areas. As you work, the meths and white spirit will break down any old polish, wax and dirt from the surface.

5. If there are any areas such as chair legs and joints, use a toothbrush. Dip it into the mixture and work it into these areas.

6. Never saturate the wood because it can warp or buckle when wet. Allow it to fully dry naturally for at least a couple of hours.

7. I then use ultra-fine steel wool wire to remove any cleaning residue or dirt, working my way from top to bottom with the wood grain. The higher the number grade for the steel wool, the coarser the material. 0000 is the finest grade and ideal for buffing and cleaning.

Cleaning outdoor furniture

A lot of outdoor furniture is made from teak because it is sustainable and offers excellent value for money. It also has loads of natural oils, so it is well-protected from the elements and very long-lasting. Over time, it will lighten, start gathering dirt and change colour from a golden brown to a silver grey.

You can use special cleaners, but I prefer using white vinegar, which is a natural disinfectant and non-toxic.

What you need

- Hard-bristled brush
- White vinegar
- Teak oil

How to clean your furniture

1. Mix 120ml of vinegar with 4 litres water.

2. Choose a sunny day and gently scrub down the furniture with the cleaning solution.

3. Concentrate on the tricky areas and see the dirt and grime disappear.

4. Rinse with cool water.

5. If there is still dirt, scrub the areas again.

6. Once it is fully dry and clean, use special teak oil to restore the oils in the wood and to protect the furniture from the elements.

FURNITURE CARE

It is important that all furniture is cared for so it lasts for many years. Here are just a few of my top tips:

Regular dusting

If you do not dust or wipe wooden furniture, the particles can form a layer that might damage the surface of the wood if it is not finished. Use a feather duster or cotton cloth to dust the item gently. If it needs more of a clean, use a cloth with water and a mild detergent like washing-up liquid to wipe it down. Never soak wooden furniture or use any cloth that is too abrasive. Little and often is best!

Avoid humidity

Try to keep your furniture in a well-ventilated room by regularly opening the windows. When the air is humid, the wood will absorb water, causing damage such as shrinking or swelling. When I first started working, there was a client who kept moving his furniture to the Philippines and back, and it needed constant restoration. I must've restored one sideboard about four times. If you have a much-loved item and are in a humid environment, a de-humidifier could help.

Careful with central heating

Like humidity, fluctuations in temperature can cause issues such as lifting veneers and cracking. It is recommended that any antique furniture be kept around $\frac{1}{2}$ metre from radiators and other heat sources. Furniture tends to find its equilibrium within a certain environment, but moving it from place to place can be problematic.

Keep away from direct sunlight

If your furniture is in direct sunlight, the finish can fade or become discoloured. Ideally, antiques should be in a dark, cool room, but that's not that practical! It's just important to be mindful and not place it right next to a window where the sun is shining all day.

Use coasters and placemats

Spills and ring marks happen all the time. One of the best ways to avoid this is to use plenty of mats and coasters on tables and sideboards to prevent these issues. There are also a couple of quick fixes for removing watermarks that I will talk about later in the book (see page 58). A bit like carpets, the sooner you tackle any stain on wooden furniture, the better.

Wax or polish regularly

Regular waxing or polishing will help protect the wood and stop damage in its tracks. In theory, a lot of older furniture should already be waxed or finished, but after years of use and gentle cleaning, the finish will start to be removed. When cleaning, avoid harsh cleaning sprays – some may melt through the polish or remove the patina. Every couple of months or so, go over your furniture with wax.

QUICK
FIXES

Beautiful old furniture has been made to last, so trying to repair it when it is damaged makes sense. You do not need years of experience to fix furniture, I promise! There are many simple and quick ways to fix damage to wooden surfaces using items you have at home or a small number of bought products. The technique you use will depend on the type and extent of the damage. Sometimes, imperfections can be left and will simply form part of the unique character of your furniture, but more often than not, small imperfections can be easily fixed.

WATERMARKS

Watermarks can normally be recognised by their distinctive white colour. These patches are known as 'blooming', where moisture has become trapped inside the polish.

If it's a new stain, it will be easier to remove it yourself. Ideally, you need to extract the water from the surface quickly for the best results. There are inexpensive ring-removing products that you can buy from hardware stores that draw the water out. If the water has gone through the polish, you may have to re-finish it.

Using an iron to remove watermarks

—

One way I remove watermarks that are still damp is by using an iron. I think it works for me at least 95 per cent of the time!

What you need

- Piece of thick kitchen towel or clean, soft cotton cloth
- Iron

How to remove the watermark

1. Start by laying a piece of kitchen towel or a cloth over the mark.

2. Set your iron to a low temperature.

3. Once it is warm, briefly rest the tip of the iron over the kitchen towel on top of the watermark.

4. Keep moving the iron and lifting it up to ensure you do not make a mark.

5. Peel back the cloth between touches to ensure it is working.

6. The iron should effectively evaporate the moisture in the wood, restoring it to its original appearance.

Using mayonnaise to remove watermarks
—

Did you know you could remove watermarks with the mayonnaise in your fridge? The oil in the mayonnaise will displace the moisture in the watermark, making this an easy quick fix. Only use this on finished wood, like French polish, or else you will just end up with oily wood.

What you need

- Piece of thick kitchen towel
- Jar of mayonnaise – any brand will do!
- Clean, soft cotton cloth

How to remove the watermark

1. Using a piece of kitchen towel, gently blot mayonnaise onto the watermark.

2. Let it sit for a few hours, and leave the towel on top.

3. Simply wipe away and buff with a clean cloth.

SCRATCHES

Wooden furniture can become scratched really easily. From kids doing their homework on the table and making a mark to knocking a sideboard by mistake on the way past, the odd scratch is part of the wear and tear of everyday life.

Removing a scratch using wax sticks
—

I love using wax sticks for a variety of jobs because they are so easy to handle. The idea of disguising a scratch on an otherwise undamaged surface is not to completely hide it, but to take the eye away from it because the scratch will look like it is part of the grain.

What you need

- Wax sticks
- Fine steel wool wire
- Kitchen foil
- Lighter
- Flat-bladed knife
- Fine sandpaper
- Polish pad and polish
- Spirit-based stain or pigment (see page 103)
- Fine brush
- Wax
- Clean, soft cotton cloth

How to remove the scratch

1. Find a coloured wax stick roughly the same shade as the furniture – there are loads available. If you can't get exactly the right colour you are looking for, blend two sticks together to get the right tint.

2. Remove the surface wax by rubbing it with fine steel wool.

3. Crumble some of the wax stick onto a piece of foil and heat it underneath with a lighter so it melts – I make up about 2 teaspoons worth.

4. Once it has melted, gently drip the wax into the scratch, using a flat-bladed knife to direct it in.

5. Allow the melted wax to harden, then remove the excess on the surface with the knife.

6. Remove the last traces of wax with fine sandpaper.

7. Charge a polish pad with polish and go over the scratched area to seal in the wax and blend it in.

8. If you are feeling really creative, mix a spirit-based stain or pigment to match the original surface and apply it to the surface. Leave it to dry.

9. Now mix a slightly darker spirit-based stain or pigment and apply it to the scratch with a fine brush to imitate the wood grain pattern, helping it to blend into the surrounding area.

10. Leave to dry, then add another layer of polish with your pad.

11. Once dry, buff the whole area with some wax using your cloth and admire your handiwork!

Removing a scratch using a walnut

Another way you can remove scratches from lighter-coloured and lightly scratched wood is by using a walnut.

What you need

- Walnut
- Clean, soft cotton cloth

How to remove the scratch

1. Simply rub the walnut back and forth diagonally over the wood.

2. Rub the scratched areas with your finger to help the wood absorb the natural oil from the walnut.

3. Wipe down and buff the area with a soft cloth.

DENTS

It is very easy to dent furniture by dropping stuff onto the surface. If you dent some chair legs, it probably won't be noticeable, so any mark is probably best left alone, but any dents on a flat tabletop or floor can be fixed using steam.

Raising a dent with an iron

When there are dents, this is because the fibres of the wood have been crushed, so ideally you need to lift them again. This can often be successfully done using the steam and heat from an iron. This will only work if the piece of furniture has not lost wood and it is just crushed rather than chipped. It also can only be used on solid wood rather than veneered wood.

What you need

1. Water
2. Thick kitchen towel or clean, soft cotton cloth
3. Iron
4. Methylated spirits
5. Fine steel wool wire
6. Fine sandpaper
7. Stain
8. Polish or wax

How to remove the dent

1. Drip a small amount of water into the dent.

2. Cover it with a piece of kitchen towel or damp cloth (always squeeze out the cloth before placing it on the wood so it is not soaked through).

3. Let the water rest so it can penetrate the fibres of the wood.

4. Use the tip of your iron on a low setting and pass it over the kitchen towel or cloth.

5. Keep moving it, slowly making the area you are ironing a bit bigger. The compressed fibres should start to absorb the steam and swell to fit their original space, so the dent will disappear.

6. Keep lifting the cloth and if the dent is still there, make the iron slightly hotter and repeat the process.

7. If you have made a watermark, use a dry cloth and run the iron over.

8. If there is localised damage, wash the areas of damaged polish using methylated spirits and fine steel wool.

9. Use fine sandpaper to smooth down any imperfections or discolouration – always sand in the direction of the grain using light strokes.

10. If the area is lighter than the surrounding areas, you may need to use a stain to help disguise it further.

11. Finish with polish or wax.

STAINS

There are different ways to remove stains from wooden furniture. Some people use bicarbonate of soda or washing-up liquid. Others even swear by toothpaste! My favourite product to use is something called Bar Keepers Friend.

Removing a stain using Bar Keepers Friend

Bar Keepers Friend is made from Oxalic acid, which is naturally found in rhubarb and spinach. Not only is it great for cleaning rust, it's also great for removing a variety of stains from wood, including ink. It never leaves any trace, but you must ensure it is localised, as it can cause discolouration.

Bar Keepers Friend is an abrasive. Always wear gloves if applying it with a cloth as it can irritate your skin. It's also not to be used on cast iron, granite, marble, wood, fabric, leather, or painted surfaces.

What you need

- Clean, soft cotton cloths
- Bar Keepers Friend
- Cotton buds
  (for small stains)
- Water

How to remove the stain

1. Wipe over the surface with a moist cloth to remove any dirt.

2. Mix 1 tablespoon of Bar Keepers Friend with a little water to make a consistency that is like toothpaste.

3. Add the mixture to a cloth.

4. Wipe the stained areas of wood with the cloth – if it is really small, use a cotton bud for accuracy.

5. Keep wiping until all traces of the stain are removed – the instructions advise that the product should be left on the wood for no longer than a minute.

6. Wipe over the area with a damp and clean cloth.

7. Leave the item to dry.

WILL'S TIP

I am applying Bar Keeper's
Friend with a brush here,
please remember to use
gloves if you use decide to use
a cloth to apply it to furniture.

REPAIRING VENEER

There is a huge variety of veneers and veneer cuts used for both antique and modern furniture. Popular types of veneer include mahogany, walnut and satinwood, which can be highly decorative. I have hundreds of pieces of veneer stored in my workshop and could write another whole book about it. Veneer damage is quite common in old furniture because it is thin and delicate.

Repairing loose veneer

Repairing loose veneer is a similar process to banishing a blister (see page 76). This method is best if the damage is localised. If a larger area of veneer is lifting, the veneer may need to be removed, cleaned, glued and re-clamped in its entirety, and that is not a quick fix!

What you need

- Scalpel
- PVA or woodworking glue
- Palette knife
- Clean, soft cotton cloth
- Clamp
- Cling film
- Polish or wax

How to repair the veneer

1. Insert a scalpel (or another small object) under the veneer and remove as much of the old glue and dust as possible.

2. Spread PVA or woodworking glue into the space using a palette knife; you will need to be quite generous with the glue.

3. Press the veneer down smoothly a number of times to spread the glue as evenly as you can into the space.

4. Remove any excess glue with a damp cloth.

5. Cover the veneer with cling film, clamp it into place and leave for a day or two until the glue hardens. The cling film acts as a barrier, preventing the clamp from sticking to the veneer.

6. Polish or wax the entire surface.

Repairing chipped veneer

Chipped veneer can feel like it might turn into a bigger problem at any moment. Wax sticks are an easy solution to any chips or cracks in your veneer. The process is the same as for removing a scratch (see page 63), except you need to build the wax stick up more so it completely fills any chip. You may need to use two colours – one for the base and then a darker colour for the grain.

What you need

- Clean, soft cotton cloth
- Wax sticks
- Kitchen foil
- Lighter
- Palette knife
- Fine sandpaper
- Polish pad and polish

How to repair the veneer

1. Use a soft cloth to clean the chipped area and remove any dust or dirt in the chip.

2. Choose a wax stick that closely matches the colour of your veneer. If you cannot find an exact match, you may need to blend two colours together.

3. Soften the wax by putting it on foil and gently heating it from underneath with the lighter. Do not overheat, as the wax needs to be pliable.

4. Carefully fill the chipped area with softened wax. Press the wax into the chip using a palette knife. Make sure it is slightly higher than the surface of the item.

5. Once dry, use knife to remove any excess wax.

6. Use the fine sandpaper to gently blend the waxed area into the surrounding veneer.

7. Apply polish to finish the area.

WILL'S TIP

Sometimes I use masking tape as a mixing pallet for glues and colour matching. You can make it to any size, it won't move around whilst you're mixing, and you can throw it away after use.

BLISTERS

Blisters are due to veneered surfaces lifting because the glue bond holding them in place has failed due to water, heat or age.

Repairing a blister using glue

What you need

- **❶** Water
- **❷** Small sharp knife or blade
- **❸** PVA glue
- **❶** Clean, soft cotton cloth
- **❷** Cling film
- **❸** Wooden block
- **❶** Clamp
- **❷** Polish pad and polish
- **❸** Wax

How to remove a blister

1. Using a sharp knife or blade, make a small incision into the blistered piece of veneer in the direction of the grain so it is disguised.

2. Drip a bit of water onto the incision.

3. Work a small bit of PVA glue into the incision using your finger or a knife – the glue will find the water, and this helps draw it into the space between the veneer and the core.

4. Wipe away the excess glue with a cloth.

5. Place some cling film over the blister. Lay a wooden block on top and fix it in place with a clamp. I didn't use cling film to do this at university and glued the wooden block to the veneer! Don't make this mistake ...

6. Leave it for 24 hours to allow the veneer to re-bond with the core of the wood.

7. Remove the clamp and wooden block.

8. Rub off any excess glue with a wet cloth.

9. Charge your polish pad, as in the opposite image, and add a thin layer of polish and wax to the treated area and surrounding surface.

FINISHES

Wooden furniture is finished in different ways for varying reasons. Finishes can enhance the furniture's look and highlight the grain patterns and colours, giving it a more vibrant look. Finishing will also add a protective layer to the surface to shield it from minor scratches, dirt and environmental factors, like moisture. It will make furniture easier to maintain, so if you spill a glass of red wine or Ribena, it will not stain the wood. Finishing can also make furniture smoother to handle.

The finish will be designed to bring out these unique properties. Across different periods, there are often preferences for different aesthetic effects and designs, such as a glossy, matt or distressed appearance. Historically, certain finishes may be used for specific types of furniture according to historical best practices.

The finishes we use today on furniture are exactly the same as those used for hundreds of years to protect, feed and enhance the appearance of the wood. Every antiques and restoration expert will have their preferred techniques and methods. I love French polishing beautiful items; it is hard work, but the results are always worth it.

Wood polishing specifically focuses on improving the shine and lustre of a wooden surface. This is primarily a cosmetic procedure, whereas waxing offers a protective barrier and enhances the wood's colour and grain. I will also cover oiling, which nourishes wood and brings out its colour, as well as staining, pigments and mould-making.

Preparing wood before finishing

When painting or polishing a wooden surface, preparation is always key. Any contaminants such as wax, dirt or grease can act as a barrier, preventing whatever you are applying from sticking to the surface or causing a reaction like bubbling or crazing. Start by cleaning your furniture using my furniture cleaner (see page 46).

Before polishing furniture, I always try to make sure the surface is smooth. The smoother the surface is, the better the polish will sit on it. I go through various grades of sandpaper, from medium or fine grit to ultra-fine grit. This ensures that it will remove any surface contaminants as well as scratches. A good sanding technique is easy to learn and it will make it easier to sand tight corners and contours.

What you need
- Goggles and mask
- Sanding block
- 120, 240 and 320-grit sandpaper
- Clean, soft cotton cloth

WILL'S TIP

If you are finishing an item of furniture that has not been polished or finished before, you will need to sand it back. If you have an old piece of furniture with years of polish, do not sand it back because everything, including the patina and shine, will be removed. To freshen it up, simply clean it. If you need to remove layers of polish from an item of furniture, remove one at a time using white or methylated spirits rather than waxing. to minimise damage to the colour.

How to sand a furniture item

1. Protect your eyes and lungs with goggles and a mask.

2. Wrap the 120-grit sandpaper around the sanding block, with the rough side facing outwards. The sanding block will keep the pressure even, rather than the pressure going through your fingers and creating an uneven finish. It also prevents your sandpaper from slipping or bunching up.

3. Sand all over your piece with 120-grit sandpaper to remove all the obvious dents and scratches. To avoid damage to the wood fibres, always sand in the direction of the grain. If you sand across the grain, this may leave obvious scratches.

4. Move on to your 240-grit sandpaper and repeat, using a damp cloth to remove any excess dust.

5. Repeat with the 320-grit sandpaper for a smooth and almost glass-like finish. The smoother your surface, the better it will polish up.

WAXING

All wooden furniture will need to be waxed to add a layer of protection from moisture and environmental damage. Waxing feeds the wood and helps draw out the natural colours and patinas. Wax is not a finish coat on its own but is used over an existing finish, such as polish.

Wood waxes have been around for hundreds of years and, historically, natural beeswax has been one of the most common types of wax. I like using waxes with carnauba wax, a hard wax made from the leaves of Brazilian palm trees. It is quite hard, so it can be buffed into a really shiny surface when dry.

There are loads of secret wax recipes out there and types of wax finishes. Sometimes, I will make my own wax for a unique item of furniture that needs a specific hardness, but furniture wax you can buy over the counter is fine to use.

How to wax a furniture item

What you need

- Clean, soft cotton cloths
- Wax
- Soft brush

Waxing a flat surface

1. Use a soft cloth with a thin layer of your chosen wax.

2. Apply the wax in a circular motion evenly across the surface, finishing with long and steady strokes in the direction of the grain.

3. Once the wax has hardened, use a soft clean cloth to buff the surface – again, go in the direction of the grain using smooth motions, working from one end to the other.

Waxing a carved surface

1. Apply a thin layer of wax to the surface using either a cloth or a brush to reach every part of the decoration.

2. Use a brush to even out the wax and remove any excess.

3. Allow the wax to harden, and buff the area with a soft cloth.

FRENCH POLISHING

French polishing is a technique that applies thin layers of shellac polish to wooden furniture. It achieves a stunning finish that brings out the true colour and enhances the appearance of the wood. I always think of a shiny piano that is so flat that the surface is super-reflective. Shellac comes from a resin secreted by the Lac beetle. It is dissolved in spirit and applied layer by layer to give the item a smooth and glossy appearance.

French polishing was first developed in France and has been around for hundreds of years. Traditionally, French polishing was done to show off the furniture and the wood it was made from, such as rosewood, mahogany and walnut. It is a long, slow and painstaking process, but the results can be amazing.

I have French polished so many pieces over the years and when they are finished, it always feels fantastic. A couple of years ago, I French polished a century-old rosewood tea caddy on *The Repair Shop*. Now, that was an item I would love to use for my daily cuppa!

Making a French polish pad

Creating a proper French polish pad – sometimes called a rubber or dabber – is crucial when applying shellac to antique furniture.

What you need

- Cotton wadding
- Clean, soft cotton cloth
- Container

1. Take a 15cm square of cotton wadding and fold it in half, forming a triangle by folding diagonally.

2. Reshape the cotton wadding into a pear shape with a smooth, flat sole. This is the core of your polish pad when you hold it between your fingers.

3. Cut a 25cm square of cotton cloth (old bedsheets are ideal) and place the wadding firmly in the centre so its edges are parallel with the edges of the cloth.

4. Fold the cloth in half (North to South) over the pad, forming a point. Repeat the fold with the remaining two corners (East to West) and turn the ends under the core of the pad.

5. Hold the pad in one hand, pull the excess cloth tightly, and twist the loose ends to tighten the pad.

6. Fold the twisted ends of the cloth over the pad to create a handgrip, ensuring a smooth and crease-free sole.

7. When you are not using it, store your pad in a sealed container to prevent it from drying out and becoming hard.

How to French polish

What you need

- Shellac polish
- French polish pad
  (see page 90)
- Ultra-fine steel wool wire
  or ultra-fine sandpaper
  (such as 320-grit)
- Clean, soft cotton cloth

Before you start

1. Remove all handles, fittings, hinges and other fixtures.

2. Clean the item and remove all stains. Any imperfections will be very obvious under French polish, unlike other finishes.

3. Check it over for any veneer that has come loose or other issues that may affect your French polishing.

4. Ensure it is dry and free from dirt and dust.

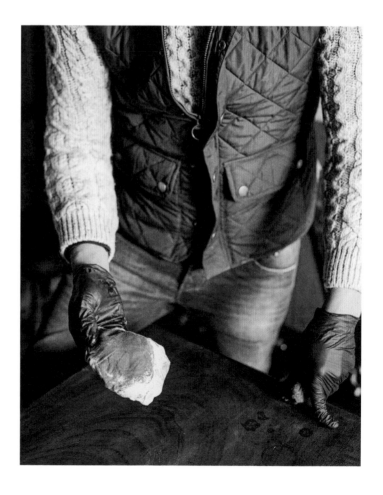

How to French polish

1. Make sure you are in a clean room and you have enough space to work.

2. Apply the shellac polish to your pad and tighten it to remove any surplus polish. Do not dip the pad in the polish.

3. As you apply the polish, always start at the edge of the piece of furniture and work along the grain. Do not lift the pad until you reach the opposite end of the surface, to avoid excess polish accumulating in the corners.

4. It can take time to perfect French polishing movements, and the idea is that it should be random strokes to create a completely flat surface. I use a mix of straight strokes following the grain, figure-of-eight motions and small and wide circles. You may like to apply a few layers of polish in one movement before changing. Try to keep the pressure light and even as you polish.

5. Once you have applied a few layers of polish, leave your furniture for at least an hour to dry. The thinner the coats, the quicker they will take to dry.

6. Use ultra-fine steel wool wire or very fine sandpaper to lightly remove any blemishes or dust on the surface of your furniture.

7. Repeat this process a number of times until you have a substantial build-up of polish on the wood. It typically takes around six to eight repetitions of the steps above before achieving a glossy or lustrous finish. After the last application, leave the item of furniture to fully dry for 24 hours.

8. Once finished, buff your item with a soft cloth and admire your handiwork.

WILL'S TIP

Hold your hand above the wood – if you can see the reflection in the surface, the job is done! On *The Repair Shop*, I get the cameraman to angle his camera so he can film my face directly in the surface – it is called a 'mirror finish'.

FURNITURE PIGMENTS AND STAINS

Wood staining involves applying a coat of stain to match or change a piece of furniture's colour or accentuate the grain. It is done to bring the piece of wood back to its original appearance.

The majority of stains are water or spirit based. Occasionally, I will use oil-based stains, but these are heavy and thick and sit on the surface of the wood, masking a lot of what is underneath. If you need a block of colour and heavy protection, these are ideal. They also offer a longer lifespan, and the finish is less likely to crack or blister.

Water-based or spirit-based stains get into the wood itself and can be diluted, so they are more translucent and you can see the grain and charm of the wood more clearly. They are used to colour in repairs or where the wood has been bleached.

Spirit-based stains dry more quickly, so they are not ideal for larger areas because they will dry before you have completed the job and this could make the appearance uneven. These are normally applied after polishing. Applying polish over the stain may result in the spirit within the polish diluting the stain and causing the surface colour to lighten.

Water-based stains are slower-drying, so they are better for larger areas. Typically, they are applied before polishing. They can sometimes raise the grain, and it will need to be sanded before progressing further. It is worth noting that both water- and spirit-based stains can be thinned after application by incorporating additional water or spirit. This means you can really build the colour up so it matches exactly the look you are hoping to achieve.

Stains can be bought in colour powder form and go a long way, so making your own stains is a very inexpensive way of restoring furniture. They are really easy to mix. I keep my stain powders in old-school plastic film canisters, and they last for absolutely ages.

Stains can be applied using a brush that will need to be carefully cleaned between uses. You can even add them to shellac polish to enhance and change the colour of your polish. It depends on the furniture you are working with and the appearance that you are trying to achieve.

Colour-matching furniture stains

There are many different types of stains and colours out there, and the process of colour-matching furniture stains to wooden items is like being an artist. I do it by eye and experience; you do not want the new colour to stick out like a sore thumb!

It can be a process of trial and error, and it can take time to perfect. I always advise keeping all your off-cuts of wood and using those to practise on or finding a similar piece to see if the stain you are planning to use is a good match by testing your stain formula on it. Clean and sand them in the same way that you have cleaned and sanded your item so they produce the same result. Keep the colour charts that you have made for future reference.

Mixing a spirit-based stain

What you need

- Glass jar
- Methylated spirits
- Stain powders
- Small teaspoon
- Brush

How to mix a spirit-based stain

1. Take a clean glass jar and pour some methylated spirits into it.

2. Add the powder to the liquid using a teaspoon. Doing it this way round will ensure there is less waste. Sometimes, I find that only a tiny pinprick of stain is needed.

3. Mix the stain solution with a brush and add more stain if needed to get to the desired colour.

4. Once you have finished working, always pour the stain away and clean your brushes. This will ensure there is no residue left that could affect the colour of future stains.

'FINISHES CAN ENHANCE
THE FURNITURE'S LOOK
AND HIGHLIGHT THE
GRAIN PATTERNS AND
COLOURS, GIVING IT
A MORE VIBRANT LOOK'

Making a stain using steel wool in a jar of white vinegar

Creating a stain using steel wool and vinegar is simple and provides a deep and dark stain, ideal for wood. Adding them together causes the steel wool to oxidise, producing a stain.

What you need

- White vinegar
- Glass jar
- Fine or ultra-fine steel wool wire
- Sieve (for straining out wool bits)

How to make the stain

1. Pour white vinegar into your jar.

2. Break up the steel wool into pieces and add to the vinegar. The finer the wool, the quicker it will break down.

3. Close your glass jar and leave the mixture to rest. The longer that you leave it, the darker the stain. Shades can vary from light grey to deep, dark brown. Depending on the stain you need, you may need to sift out the remaining steel wool.

4. Ensure your mixture is as pure as possible before working on wood. For wood with open pores, wool bits could get stuck, ruining the appearance.

WILL'S TIP

Do a test! When you apply the stain to the wood, it goes on clear and you will only see the full-colour effect when it dries. Start by applying the stain to the underside of your furniture, another hidden area or scrap wood and leave it to dry to ensure it is the colour you are looking for. If you do not like the colour, make the necessary adjustments to your mixture – either add more steel wool to make it darker or water to make it lighter.

Making stains using tea

Another idea for a non-toxic wood stain that is natural is tea. Inexpensive, non-flammable and probably in the cupboard, tea can be used to stain all types of wood, making them look richer. It reacts with the tannins in the wood to give it a consistent colour and even out any blotchiness.

It can be really fun to experiment with old and scrap pieces of different woods in varying shades.

What you need

- Tea bag (I use black tea – the darker the tea, the darker the stain will be)
- Boiled water
- Cup or glass jar
- Paintbrush
- Sealant

How to make the stain

1. Make sure your wood is clean.

2. Make a cup of tea and leave it to cool.

3. Apply the cool tea to the wood, starting on a hidden part first, using a paintbrush. You can also apply it with a rag or even the teabag itself.

4. Leave the coats to dry and keep applying the stain until you have the desired colour.

5. When dry, use a sealant to seal the stain in place.

PIGMENTS

Stains are typically translucent or semi-translucent, so they will penetrate the surface of the wood whilst changing the colour but allowing the natural grain to show through. Pigments are opaque, so they are more artificial-looking. Solid colour particles are suspended in a binder. They will completely cover a surface and mask the wood grain behind it, so these are used for imitating grain or the more intricate detailing. It's a bit like a picture – the staining is the shading, and the pigments are the finer detailing. It's important to build it up in thinner layers, as going on too thick can spoil the illusion of a natural wood grain effect.

Imitating wood grain

Acrylic paints or pigments offer an easy way to imitate wood grain on items of furniture that have been damaged. They are easy to use and relatively quick drying. They can also easily be mixed to create custom shades.

What you need

- Stain (for a base coat)
- Brushes
- Acrylic pigments that match the colour of the grain
- Rag or sponge to blend the colour in (if required)
- Wax or polish

WILL'S TIP

As well as stains for the background colour, I sometimes use watercolour paints to complete this part. Use sparingly and water down at first because these can also go a long way.

How to paint wood grain

1. Ensure your surface is free of dust and debris.

2. Use a stain for a base coat in the area that needs to be restored and ensure it is fully dry.

3. Use a fine brush to apply the pigments so you can recreate the natural pattern of the wood more clearly. Look for lines and knots to make it as realistic as possible.

4. When the paint is still wet, gently blend the detailing using a rag or sponge to mimic the wood's soft and natural appearance.

5. Allow to dry. Touch up again and build up if necessary. Leave to dry between coats.

6. Wax or polish to finish.

OILING FURNITURE

Furniture is often oiled to help protect and preserve the wood. Oiling can help rejuvenate the wood to enhance its colour and appearance. Where the grain style is a prominent design feature, oiling can help it to stand out. It will also help to nourish the wood, which is particularly important for hardwoods like mahogany and oak. Once the oil is applied, you will not need to oil it for a number of years.

There are loads of different types of oils that are often designed for specific types of wood. Having said that, I use walnut oil on other wood types, and it still looks great! I also like linseed oil because it deeply penetrates the grain and can be used alongside other finishes like wax to add another layer of protection. It is also eco-friendly and non-toxic.

What you need

- Oil
- Clean, soft cotton cloth
- Fine or ultra-fine sandpaper (240-grit or 320-grit is ideal)

WILL'S TIP

Never put your oily rag in the bin because it could spontaneously combust. Always leave your rag to dry completely outside before throwing it away.

How to oil furniture

1. Ensure your item of furniture is cleaned and sanded.

2. Apply a generous quantity of oil directly to the surface of the wood.

3. Gently rub the oil into the wood using a clean, soft cotton cloth or rag. Work in the direction of the natural grain of the wood in circular motions in clean strokes. Apply firm pressure to distribute the oil evenly.

4. Continue until the whole surface of your furniture is covered.

5. Allow the oil to remain on the wood for approximately half an hour, and then wipe the excess away.

6. Let the wood stand for a day or so. What tends to happen is that the oil will be drawn into the wood so that the top will be dry, and it will be clear that the item needs further oiling.

7. Use fine or ultra-fine sandpaper and lightly sand over the surface to raise the grain of the wood. This will help the oil soak into the furniture more easily.

8. Repeat the process as many times as you wish until the top feels completely smooth. You will know because the oil will just sit on the surface.

MOULD MAKING

Mould making is the process of making decorative mouldings or elements of your piece of furniture that have been lost or damaged to bring it back to its original condition.

Replicating these successfully is really important – not only so your item of furniture looks uniform but for historical accuracy. It can be impossible to refabricate or recurve them out of wood, so you can make a mould and cast a replica in a different material. This is then painted and glued to the item to blend in perfectly – job done!

There are different materials to mould, with varying curing times and consistencies, so experiment to find what you like working with – whether it is creating an impression from a carved gilt mirror frame that could be recreated in gesso or plaster or replacing a missing keyhole escutcheon with resin and metal powder. Mould-making kits are handy materials to have in your restoration toolbox. If I make a small mould to look like wood, I use a special wood filler that dries incredibly quickly and comes in a light brown colour. It already looks quite like wood before I start trying to make it look like the original, so I am halfway there.

What you need

- Silicone mould-making kit
- Resin casting kit
- Wood glue
- Clean, soft cotton cloth or sandpaper
- Paint and paintbrush

How to make the mould

1. Silicone-based mould-making kits come in two parts – A and B. Mix these parts equally so you have a solid and equal colour.

2. Apply the mixture to the piece that you want to mould. Work quickly because the chemical reaction between the two parts means you only have a few minutes to get the job done. Push the putty over the components and into all the crevices to get the exact shape correct. You need to recreate every aspect of the desired shape, so the whole thing will need to be totally covered.

3. Allow the mould to harden and pop out your original item from the mould.

4. Now, you need to make the part – this can be done using various casting compound materials, such as resin. Follow the instructions on the kit to make the solution and mix thoroughly.

5. Pour it into the mould, ensuring an even finish.

6. Allow the piece to cure and harden. Follow the instructions regarding waiting times.

7. Pop the piece gently out of the mould.

8. Clean your mould – it can be used again!

9. Give the item a bit of a clean or gentle sand.

10. Stick to your furniture using your wood glue.

11. Paint and finish.

WILL'S TIP

If I am making a mould to replicate a metal item, like a keyhole, I add bronze or metal-look powders to my resin to help match the original. Once it is dry, I also use fine steel wool wire to rub on the surface, and it shines up and makes the item look like metal.

LARGER PROJECTS

n this chapter, I will show you how I have completed three restorations. I deliberately chose three different items with varying requirements. The first item is a child's chair, as I always used to receive loads of chairs in my workshop. The second is a side table I restored for my hallway, and the third is a sideboard.

Before I was on *The Repair Shop*, when I spent more time in my workshop, autumn was often the busiest time of year for me. This was because people used to unearth all their furniture so their friends and family could sit around the table at Christmas, and they would realise that the chair had a wobbly leg or the table had a chip in it. The items that tended to come in were the ones that saw the most wear and tear over the years and where the joints had failed – a sign of good times! These three items are very typical of that work.

Each item of furniture is unique, so I never approach a project in the same way, but here I will cover a few of the techniques I outlined earlier in the book, as well as a few new ones.

NINETEENTH-CENTURY ANTIQUE MAHOGANY LADDERBACK CHILD'S CHAIR

This is a lovely chair with huge potential. I saw it on eBay. It caught my eye because it's quite unusual and just the sort of item that would look lovely alongside more contemporary furniture in a child's bedroom. I love children's chairs; we bought my daughter a chair when she was born and have taken a picture of her every month propped up in it, and I love looking back at them.

There are two things that I look at when I first inspect an item. Firstly, I examine the structure. Are there joints that are broken? Is anything missing from the structure? What wood is it made out of? Then I think about the aesthetics. Is there surface damage? What sort of patination does it have? Does it need to be re-waxed or French-polished?

On first inspection of this chair, I could see it was mahogany due to its colour and age. It was clear that most of the damage had occurred around the area where the arm meets the back of the chair. A screw hole had been made during its construction, creating a weakness. It must have broken a few times in the past, as I could see someone had tried to repair it with additional nails and screws, further weakening the wood until it became almost irreparable. This meant that much of the chair's back had come away from the main structure.

The polish on the surface had become dull. What should have been a warm mahogany colour instead had a grey and lifeless look. The seat panel could also easily be replaced to give the chair a more contemporary feel. I knew that with a little TLC, this wonderful chair could have a new lease of life.

First steps

I started by cleaning the surface of the chair with my homemade furniture cleaner (see page 46). This not only removes the surface dirt and prepares it for polishing, but it will also reveal any hidden further damage lying beneath the surface. When cleaning, I started from one side and methodically worked around the chair to ensure nothing was missed. If you plan to French polish a surface, it will need to be incredibly clean because if there is any residue, the polish will not stick.

Once the chair and the parts that had come away had been cleaned, I removed all traces of old wood glue from the different joints. For the two wooden surfaces to glue back together properly, both sides need to be free from any contaminants, including dust, dirt, wax and old glue. I always start with the least invasive method first to avoid unnecessary damage. One effective way of removing old glue is to wet the area with warm water and use a small brush to work it into the surface.

I then used a heat gun to heat the glue gently. As the glue warms, it turns into a softer chewing gum consistency; this makes it a lot easier to remove without the risk of damaging or picking out the surrounding wood by mistake. I then used a small chisel to pick out the loose glue.

WILL'S TIP

I use an old toothbrush
because it is small enough
to get into the tight areas,
and the bristles are coarse
enough to work the water
into the glue.

Next steps

My next task was to cut out and remove the damaged areas of wood. It can be tricky to restore old chairs, as previous restoration work could be hiding unexpected screws and nails beneath the surface, so I always go easy when starting to saw or chisel. Most nail or screw holes would have been filled in with a furniture wax stick, so it is always good to have a look around for them as you might be able to unscrew them or remove the nails, making it easier to dismantle the chair.

Once I was happy there were no hidden surprises, I started to saw out the damaged sections. My plan was to only cut halfway through the wood, allowing me to 'sandwich' a new piece of mahogany in place, almost like a tailor-made puzzle piece. I used my thin Japanese saw; the blade is very sharp, allowing me to make surgical incisions. This let me remove the damaged wood, ready for new wood.

I glued and clamped new pieces of mahogany on the front, back and top corner of the back rail. Even though I made them to a snug fit, I intentionally left excess wood around the outside edges. This would give me more wiggle room when shaping them to match their surrounding area.

Having left the glue to dry overnight, I used a combination of a saw, a sharp chisel and a hand plane to remove the excess wood, blending the new wood into the original surrounding areas. The damage to the corner of the carved top rail was slightly trickier to restore. On one hand, I could use the carving on the other side for reference, as the design is symmetrical. However, on the other hand, if I was not able to precisely shape it, it would catch your eye and stick out like a sore thumb. After carefully marking out the pattern on the face of the new section of wood, I then used my wood rasps to shape in the detail. Once all the woodwork had been completed, I finished the new areas with a light sand, starting with 240 grit sandpaper for some final shaping and finishing off with 320 grit for a smooth finish.

WILL'S TIP

When using metal clamps, I often put a small off-cut of wood or cardboard between the clamp and the wooden surface to protect it, unless I'm using a clamp that already has rubber pads.

How to use wood rasps
—

Wood rasps are hand tools used for roughly shaping wood before more intensive shaping with other tools. Wood rasps either have flat, narrow or rounded surfaces with teeth for quick wood removal.

Select the right rasp for the task in hand – flat rasps are better for larger surfaces, whilst rounded rasps are better for curved surfaces. Secure the piece of wood that you are working with. Apply gentle and even pressure while pushing the rasp across the surface of the wood in a forward motion. If you need to go against the grain, go gently because this could end up damaging the wood. Frequently check to see the progress you are making and make adjustments as needed to achieve the desired shape.

WILL'S TIP

If you are rasping a large piece of wood, regularly use a wire brush to remove the debris from the teeth of the rasp because this can reduce its effectiveness.

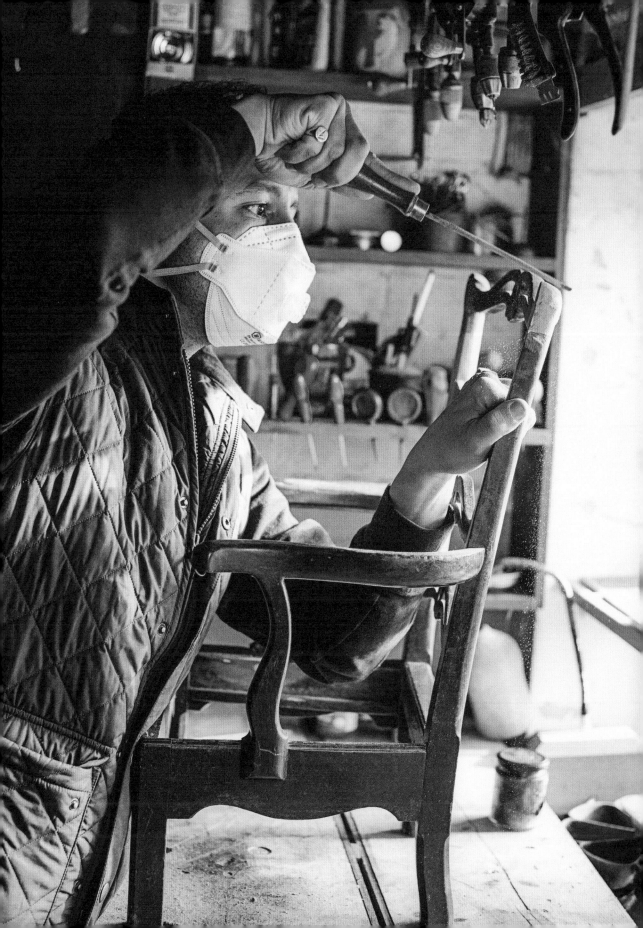

The new wood was much lighter than the rest of the original chair and needed colour-matching to blend everything. Even though they are both the same species of wood, the younger, faster-grown mahogany called Sapele that I used to patch the chair is lighter in colour. I started by applying a thin coat of polish to the entire chair. This is always recommended when polishing a new piece of wood because it raises the grain when it dries, creating a rough surface, and, once it is lightly sanded back, it creates the perfect sealed smooth surface for polishing or waxing. Importantly, the colour of the wood will look completely different when it is unfinished compared to when polished, so this will show me the final colour of the wood that I'll be trying to match.

I used an off-cut of mahogany as a test panel to help me mix up and recreate the original colour of the chair. As mentioned earlier in the book, it is always a good idea to test your pigments, stains and polish on a scrap of wood or a hidden or discreet area, such as the underside of the furniture, before moving on to the main area, reducing the risk of damaging the rest of the furniture.

I tested the stain on the underside of the chair. Fortunately, my 'Dark Oak' spirit stain was the perfect colour-match, and I used it with a mix of shellac polish and a medium artist's brush to blend all the woodwork together.

Finishing touches

The finish of a piece of furniture is subjective and comes down to the look you are aiming for. The chair could have been finished with shellac or a full French polish, which would look glossy, or a waxed finish, where the steel wool removes the 'candy-coated' shine and works the wax into the surface. For this chair, once the stain had fully dried, I sealed it in and polished the entire chair with a few thin coats of shellac. Once buffed, the shellac created a subtle sheen whilst still enhancing the colour and lustre. In order to create a brushmark-free finish, I applied the polish with a French polish pad to leave the piece of furniture with a flawless finish. Having left the polish to cure overnight, I finally finished the woodwork with a brown furniture wax. This was applied with fine steel wool and buffed with a cotton cloth.

Having finished the main body of the chair, I decided to re-cover the seat. The fabric was in good shape, though I wanted to update it for more of a modern look. Being a drop-in seat meant that rather than the upholstery being attached directly to the chair itself, it was instead fitted onto a separate wooden frame that sits on top of the chair frame, making it much easier to re-cover.

Having removed the old upholstery tacks and fabric, I could see that the stuffing on the inside was in decent condition, so only a replacement top cover was needed. After ironing and roughly cutting the fabric to size, I began to apply new tacks around the underside edge. Starting with a single tack in the centre of each side allowed me to make any minor adjustments to the layout of the fabric and tautness until I was happy enough to add the rest of the tacks and neaten the edges by removing the final excess fabric. Once the seat was in place, the item was ready to go. I was delighted with how it looked.

Re-covering a seat pad

I am not an upholsterer, but I am always happy to re-cover a seat pad when the stuffing is in good condition. I think this can be a really simple and quick way to transform the look of an item of furniture and a very cheap way to make a chair look smarter or add a pop of colour to a room.

   I use special furniture tacks, but some people choose to use a staple gun.

What you need

- Pliers/small chisel
- Iron
- Pencil
- Scissors
- Furniture tacks
- Small hammer

How to re-cover a seat pad

1. Start by removing the seat from the chair. If it is not a drop-in seat, you may need to unscrew it. Make the necessary repairs to the seat frame, such as tightening joints or refinishing, before you put the finished seat back in the chair.

2. Gently remove the old tacks using pliers or a chisel.

3. Save the old fabric to use as a pattern.

4. Iron the new fabric to make sure it is completely flat.

5. Mark the shape in the new fabric using the old seat cover as a guide, noting the location of the tacks.

6. Cut out the new fabric using the guides you have just made.

7. Turn the new seat cover upside down and place the seat cushion on top of it.

8. Starting with the middle tack on each side, gently hammer the tacks into position.

9. Keep pulling the fabric taut, smoothing the material from the centre as you place the other tacks into position, leaving the corners until last.

10. Pull one corner of the fabric towards the centre of the seat, placing the tack into position with a smooth, flat finish.

11. Complete the other three corners.

12. Place the seat back on the chair frame and re-attach if necessary.

VICTORIAN MAHOGANY TWO-DRAWER SIDE TABLE

This classic piece of Victorian furniture belonged to a friend of mine who no longer had a use for it. I'm always on the lookout for disused bits of furniture destined for landfill to either restore or use for scraps, including wood, screws and hinges. On this occasion, I knew that with a clean and polish, this piece would be perfect for my hallway.

When looking at it, I could see that one of the drawers was broken, but structurally, the piece was sound. The top also had a large dent and needed some work to restore its colour and shine.

'SOMETIMES, IMPERFECTIONS CAN BE LEFT AND WILL SIMPLY FORM PART OF THE UNIQUE CHARACTER OF YOUR FURNITURE, BUT MORE OFTEN THAN NOT, SMALL IMPERFECTIONS CAN BE EASILY FIXED'

First steps

I started by cleaning all the surfaces. The legs did not require stripping as they were in good condition, so I cleaned them with my furniture cleaner (see page 46). The top, however, was in bad shape. I always try to start with the least invasive approach when refinishing a tabletop as I like to retain as much of the character as possible. It takes years for a wooden surface to build up its charm and patination. In this case, there was hardly any depth to the polish and there were areas where it had completely worn through. I removed what was left of the polishing from the surface with methylated spirits and a cotton cloth. As tempting as it would be to sand the top down, I would then run the risk of removing all the minor scratches and dents that also give an antique its charisma.

Once cleaned, I sealed the top with a thin coat of shellac to seal the surface and reveal the true colour of the mahogany. Sometimes over-cleaning and sun bleaching can distort and change the colour of wood, but thankfully, after cleaning, the colour of the top still matched the base, so there was no need to stain it.

Next steps

Many of the scratches to the top were old and superficial, however, there was a nasty dent in the top that needed attention. It looked like someone had dropped a chisel on the table.

Often, dents can be removed using an iron and a lightly damp cloth to steam the dents out (see page 66). This technique is best used on solid top wood rather than veneered furniture, as too much heat from the iron can potentially melt the adhesive and lift the veneer from the surface. With a solid wooden top, the steam from the iron and moisture from the cloth can expand the damaged wooden fibres, almost springing them back into shape and filling out the dent. On this occasion, whatever had dropped on the surface had torn the wooden fibres, making the dent hard to steam out.

Thankfully, I keep a selection of furniture wax sticks in my toolbox. These have helped me in many tricky situations. If you can find the perfect colour-match wax stick 'right out of the box', then they can be rubbed into the scratch or dent (see page 63). If you cannot find the perfect colour, you can melt different colours together and make your own. I melted two wax sticks together and filled the hole. Any excess wax can be removed with a flat piece of plastic, ideally without sharp edges. This can also be done with a flat-bladed knife. Once the wax had set and was slightly smoothed down with fine sandpaper, I used a fine paintbrush with some brown pigment and polish to imitate the wood grain on the surface, further disguising the damage.

Even though one of the drawers was in pieces, thankfully, the dovetail joints were all still intact, so they just needed to be glued back together. I did so, running a thin line of wood glue along the joints and connecting them. Then, I taped the drawer up with masking tape and put it back into the furniture.

Once it had dried, I removed the tape and cleaned and waxed the drawer slides/runners. Over many years of use, the friction of drawers going in and out can slowly rub down the wood and create a fine sawdust powder. This, along with dust and other debris, causes the drawers to stick and stop sliding. A vacuum, a light sand with fine sandpaper and a wax with a non-scented white candlestick on both the drawer slides and the underside edges of the drawers – the surface where they both meet – will free them up and make them run smoothly. The wax is brittle, so it sits on the surface to provide a lubricating effect.

WILL'S TIP

When glueing an antique drawer back together, you would naturally be inclined to clamp it up, making sure that all the corners are square. A handy trick I learned many years ago is to glue the joints, tape them up, and then slide the drawer back into the furniture. No matter how young a piece of wooden furniture is, it is always susceptible to warping, shrinking, twisting and cracking due to fluctuations in heat and moisture. So, putting the drawer in while still malleable allows it to shape itself perfectly to the surrounding table.

Finishing touches

I finished the table with a light polish. Traditionally, this table would not have had a thick body of polish, so a couple of coats of shellac with my polishing pad was enough to protect the surface and bring out the wonderful grain in the wood. If you want a quick and easy way to revive a polished surface, you could use a burnishing cream, like T-Cut. This removes any fine scratches and buffs the surface, creating a glossy finish.

How to use burnishing cream

Burnishing cream is typically used to remove white ring marks, burn marks and watermarks and can be applied to improve the lustre and shine of finished wooden surfaces.

It is lightly abrasive, so the polish or finish on the woodwork must be thick enough to withstand the cream.

What you need

- Clean, soft cotton cloth
- Burnishing cream

1. Before applying any burnishing cream, make sure the wood surface is clean. Remove any dust, dirt or residues using a soft cloth.

2. Before applying the cream to the entire surface, test it in a small, inconspicuous area to see the results.

3. Apply the cream to a small section of the wood at a time, applying in circular motions but finishing in the direction of the grain.

4. Allow the cream to sit for a few minutes until dry, and then use a cloth to buff the surface.

MID-CENTURY MCINTOSH TEAK SIDEBOARD

I absolutely love mid-century furniture, both for its design and its aesthetics. When I recently visited a friend, my eye was immediately drawn to this beautiful piece, not only for its quality and sytle but also because of the water damage to the top.

First steps

Structurally, the sideboard was in good shape, as were the front and sides. The water or wine damage had removed the stain from various parts of the top, leaving lighter ring marks. If there were only one or two minor marks, I would have coloured them in to match the surrounding area. However, because they were quite big, including a black stain, I decided to strip the old oil and stain with paint and varnish stripper. Removing the old finish using an electric sander would have been quicker, but as the top had been veneered, there is always a risk of getting carried away and sanding through to the plywood. I felt that I had much more control with the stripper.

Once I applied the stripper, it was not long before it started to work its magic. As soon as I could see it dissolving the oil and stain, I removed the waste material with a scraper. Once I finished stripping the surface, I neutralised the top with water. This ensured no residue of stripper was left behind that might keep working.

How to use paint and varnish stripper

There are different ways to remove paint and varnish from wood, but a stripper can be useful with veneered products so you do not damage the wood. Always work in a well-ventilated area and wear the right safety clothes, including goggles and gloves. Read the manufacturer's instructions for guidelines on application and removal.

What you need

- Paintbrush
- Paint and varnish stripper
- Putty knife or scraper

1. Using a paintbrush, apply a thick and even coat of the paint and varnish stripper onto the wood surface. Make sure that the entire surface is covered in a consistent manner.

2. Allow the paint and varnish stripper to work according to the manufacturer's instructions. This usually involves letting it sit on the surface for a specified amount of time.

3. After this period, test a small area with a plastic or metal putty knife or scraper to see if the finish is soft and ready for removal.

4. Gently scrape off the softened paint or varnish using the putty knife or scraper. Work in the direction of the wood grain to avoid damaging the surface. If it is not coming away, you may need to apply another coat of stripper.

5. After removing the paint or varnish, clean the wood surface to remove any remaining residue. You may need to neutralise the surface with water to stop the chemical reaction.

6. Once the wood is clean and dry, it can be sanded and finished.

WILL'S TIP

The edge of a new metal ruler is perfect for scraping off old paint and polish as it is long enough to cover a larger surface area and flexible enough to get into a variety of areas.

Thankfully, stripping back the top removed the white watermarks. However, there was still a darker mark. Rather than an ink stain, this dark grey mark was more likely created by water trapped under a metal item. Wet metal sitting on a wooden surface can react with the tannins in the wood, creating a smoky grey/black effect. I often use a great stain remover I keep stored in my restoration toolbox called Bar Keepers Friend (see page 68). Not only is it handy for cleaning metal, but it is also great for drawing stains out of wooden surfaces.

I mixed a small amount of the powder with water until it became a toothpaste consistency. I worked the paste into the stain with an old toothbrush (funnily enough, with the same pressure you would use when brushing your teeth!) until the white paste began to change colour.

I wiped away the discoloured residue every minute or so, checking to see if the stain had lightened. Once the stain had disappeared, I cleaned the entire top with clean, warm water and left it to dry.

Next steps

I stripped the old finish from the top of the sideboard and removed the dark watermark, leaving the surface much lighter than the front and side panels, so I decided to stain it. Having tested a selection of stains on a spare sample piece of wood, I found a tin of 'Medium Mahogany' water-based stain was almost an exact match. I use the manufacturer's names for stains as a rough guide when colour-matching. In this case, the mahogany was an excellent match for the teak, but on another project, a walnut stain might work well for a dark oak table.

I chose a water-based stain because I wanted to finish the sideboard in Danish oil. Once the water stain had dried, there was no risk of the oil affecting it, whereas if I used an oil stain, there is a high chance that the finishing oil would dissolve the stain and remove it from the surface when it was being applied.

WILL'S TIP

Keep the cleaning localised to the stain, as liberal use around the surrounding area could discolour the wood.

Finishing touches

Once the water stain had fully dried, I finished and protected the
top with three coats of Danish oil. As soon as the first coat was
applied, I could see the warm richness of the stained teak revived.

The front and side panels looked slightly dull, so I gave them a light
clean with water and a mild detergent, then applied two thin coats
of oil to tie them in with the top. As a finishing touch, I coloured any
minor scratches on the legs and outer edges with a mixture of brown
umber pigment and shellac with a fine artist's brush.

PROJECTS BEFORE

PROJECTS AFTER

ESSENTIAL TOOLS

When you are ready to start woodworking, you will need some essential tools. I have picked out this selection of tools as the most hard-working and versatile items in my toolbox. Starting with the right tools will improve your experience and save time and money.

These tools have not changed for centuries, though aspects like the materials and hand grip size vary. By using a tool, you will find out what is most comfortable for you. It is a bit like Harry Potter choosing a wand!

OLD TOOLS VS NEW TOOLS

The decision to invest in either old or new tools has been an ongoing discussion between woodworkers for many years. I personally find older woodworking tools are built to a better quality than new ones. My older chisels, most of which are made from Sheffield steel, tend to keep a sharper edge for longer. I bought some cheap chisels on my first day at uni and spent my whole time sharpening them.

Aesthetically, I feel that most second-hand tools, like pliers and screwdrivers, have a charm and character to them, often fitting well in the hand. The scratches and scars from their previous lives tell their story.

I believe that with most modern tools, you get what you pay for. Much like a lot of modern furniture, cheaper tools tend to be blunter, become misshaped and break more easily due to weaker materials. Some modern pliers and snips are good for ripping nails out of furniture, but I would suggest that any tool that will be knocked about should be made from the hardest-wearing and highest-quality materials, most of which will be reflected in the cost.

There is such a wide variety of tools to be found online that it can be quite overwhelming when deciding what to invest in, but the general rule of thumb is that the higher the price, the better the quality. I would spend what you can afford. You can find second-hand tools in good condition for a relatively low cost. If you find an old tool in good condition, it has either not been used very much or is just very good, so it will always be worth the cost.

Measuring tools

Always measure twice because you only get one chance to cut, and making the wrong measurements can be an expensive mistake. Ensure that you always choose the right tools to make the measurements.

- **Metal rulers:** I keep a selection of assorted sizes to make accurate measurements.
- **Tape measure:** This is a staple tool for any woodworker. I have about 20 kicking around, and they all serve the same purpose.
- **Digital callipers:** These are great for making external, internal, depth and distance measurements.
- **Sliding bevel:** This versatile tool can be used for marking angles directly onto the woodwork, so it is handy for marking out dovetail joints. It can also be used for verifying existing angles.
- **Marking gauge:** This tool makes accurate and consistent marks on the wood. It is particularly useful for scribing line layouts, such as creating a parallel line to a reference edge or surface for consistency.
- **Woodwork square:** The trusty square is used in most woodworking projects to check the accuracy of right angles.

'OLDER ITEMS ARE INHERENTLY MORE VALUABLE, AND VIRTUALLY ANY WOODEN PIECE CAN BE RESTORED; IN MY EXPERIENCE, THE OLDER THE PIECE, THE MORE REPAIRABLE IT IS.'

Rasps/files

Various-shaped rasps and files are really good for quickly shaping or carving through wood. A smaller selection of needle files is good for fine adjustments to woodwork and metalwork.

WILL'S TIP

With heavy use, files and rasps can quickly clog up. Tapping the debris out of your workbench can damage the surface of your tool. Once, my workshop was so cold that I tapped my file on the side of my bench, and the metal shattered! A gentle clean with fine brass brass will help to keep your files and rasps in top condition.

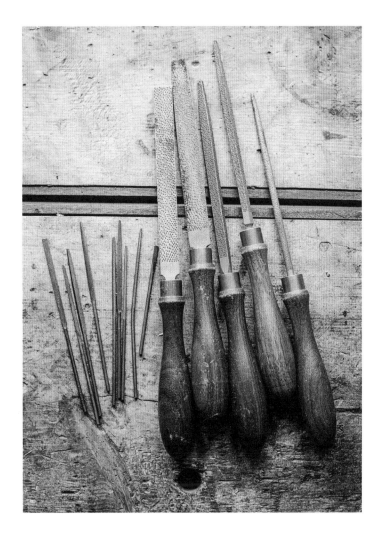

Chisels

I have a large selection of chisels, ranging from 2mm to 60mm wide, used for carving, shaping and cutting wood. My chisels have mostly been purchased for specific jobs.

For an essential set, I would suggest investing in a selection of sizes. A selection of bevel-edge chisels, 6mm (¼ inch), 10mm (³/8 inch), 13mm (½ inch), 19mm (¾ inch) and 25mm (1 inch) wide, should see you through most projects. A high-quality set will last you many years.

Pliers

Pliers are versatile tools used for gripping and holding onto smaller components, ripping out old screws and nails or for temporary clamping. Pliers can easily be bought in a set.

- **Combination pliers:** These pliers can be used for gripping and cutting through wire or cables.
- **Long nose pliers:** Also used for gripping and holding, these pliers have tapered jaws so they can reach into small spaces. They are good for detailed work, like inserting small screws or nails or removing nails or staples.
- **Cutting pliers:** These pliers are most commonly used for cutting nails close to the surface of the wood.

Sharpening stone

This tool is used to sharpen the edges of woodworking tools, such as chisels, to ensure precision and accuracy when using them. Using the stone involves running the cutting edge of the tool across the surface in a controlled way. This removes some of the material, creating a sharp edge.

I would recommend an Oilstone or Diamond stone; most are double-sided, so they provide options for two different grits. Finer grits are used for honing and polishing the edges of tools.

Planes

Planes are used for shaping, smoothing and levelling wood. There are various types of planes used for specific tasks.

- **Block plane:** This plane is great for trimming end grain and chamfered edges.
- **Smoothing plane**: This is the most commonly used plane in the workshop and is ideal for smoothing, trimming and surface finishing.

Hammers and Mallets

These essential tools have different purposes, and I always keep a selection with me.

- **Carpenter's mallet:** This wooden mallet, most commonly made from beech, is used for driving pieces of wood together, such as assembling dovetail joints. The fact it is made of wood minimises the risk of damage to the surface.
- **Rubber mallet:** This tool has a rubber head and is great for knocking wooden furniture back together without leaving dents or scratching the surface.
- **Claw hammer:** This hammer has a flat face for knocking nails into wood and a claw on the opposite side for removing them.
- **Pin hammer:** With a slender, straight claw on one end and a small, round face on the opposite side, this hammer is compact and lightweight. Pin hammers tend to be used for knocking in small pins with precision or for fine detail work.

Saws

Saws are fundamental for cutting your woodwork into the desired shape or size. Different saws have different purposes.

- **Japanese crosscut saw:** This saw is designed to make accurate and clean crosscuts across woodgrain. The design's thin blade and crosscutting teeth enable smoother cuts in contrast to Western-style saws.
- **Flush-cutting saw**: A flush-cutting saw is a tool designed for trimming protruding pieces of wood so that they are level or flush with the surrounding surface.
- **Tenon saw:** This is a handsaw used for making precise and controlled cuts. Tenon saws are frequently used for crafting the tenons utilised in mortise and tenon joints.

Screwdrivers

These tools are used for inserting and removing screws. Much like chisels, screwdrivers can range in size depending on the task they are needed for. A basic six-piece mixed Phillips and slotted set, which contains a variety of screwdrivers, each with different sizes, would get you through most tasks. Phillips screwdrivers have a cross-shaped tip, designed to fit into Phillips-head screws, whilst slotted screwdrivers have a straight, flat tip, designed for screws with a straight line slot in the head.

Combi Drill and Drill Bits/ Screwdriver Bits

Power tools are fast and efficient and have revolutionised woodworking. Drills have come a long way over the last decade and are always a popular choice to drive screws and nails into wood or metal and take them out again. Even though the old, heavy-duty plug-in drill I inherited from my dad is a great backup, most modern cordless combi drills have excellent battery life and are small and light enough to get into tricky areas. The bits refer to the interchangeable tips you can use for different tasks. They come in varying shapes and sizes to match the different types of screws.

Clamps

Many restoration projects require clamps to secure and hold woodworking items in place, but there are many types of clamps in varying sizes. I would start by buying a clamp that you need for a specific task and build your selection from there.

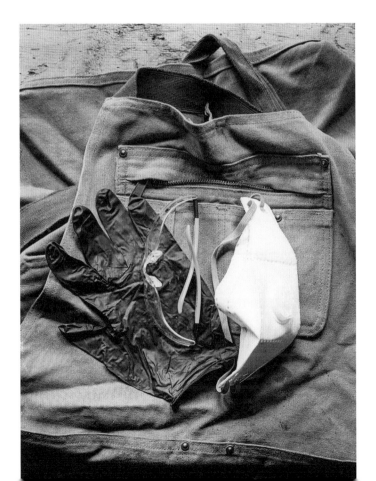

Brushes

Brushes are essential for applying stains and acrylics. Like an artist, it is just a case of choosing the right brush for the job. Brushes for applying stains will have softer bristles to allow for better absorption of the stain, whereas brushes for finer detail work will have finer bristles for a precise finish.

Having a small variety of brushes in your woodworking toolbox will allow you to tackle different tasks effectively. I have a selection of squirrel hair brushes, which are perfect for adding a coat of shellac polish to some antique furniture. They are rather expensive but extremely soft, which helps to create a flawless polished finish.

When you have finished using brushes, always clean them out with meths and store them flat, as keeping them facing brush-down in a jar of polish could destroy the neatly pointed tip, as well as ruin the hairs. Many years ago, I left a lovely brush in a jar of polish for a few weeks. When I came to use it again, I did not realise the polish had completely dried, bonding the brush to the inside of the jar. With one quick tug, the brush handle came away, leaving the brush head forever imprinted in the polish, almost like the mosquitos in *Jurassic Park* that were immortalised in amber! I've never made the same mistake again.

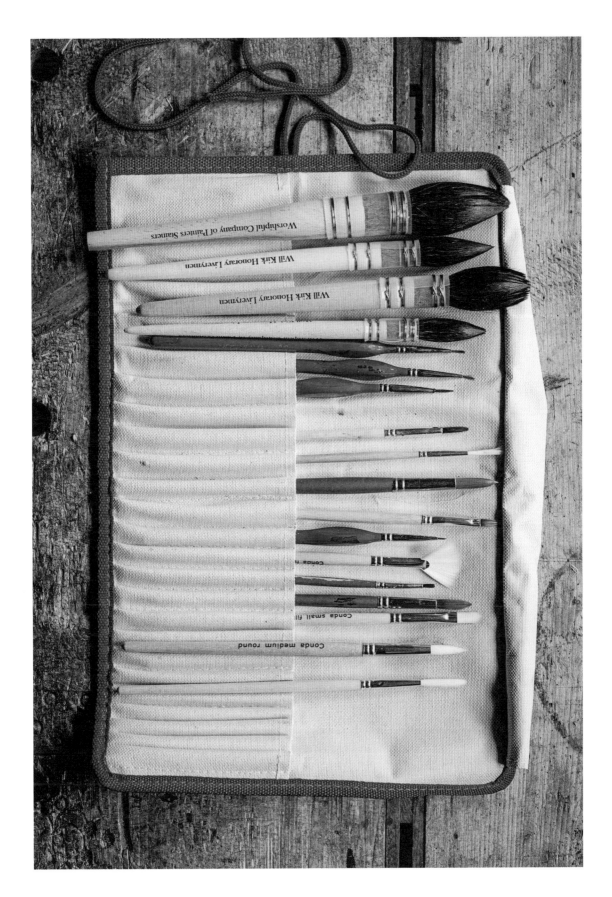

INDEX

Acknowledgements

I would like to say a massive thank you to the Ebury Publishing team who it has been an absolute pleasure to work with. The wonderful, Phoebe Lindsley, Abby Watson, Morgana Chess, Antony Heller and Céline Nyssens for believing in me and this project. A special thanks to Albert DePetrillo, who could see the potential in this book and gave me the confidence to share my love of woodworking on paper.

Thank you to my patient, reassuring ghost writer, Georgina Rodgers for making sense of my scrambled thoughts and ideas. You have been integral in helping to bring this project to life.

I wanted this book to not only inform, but also to look wonderful sitting on a coffee table. Next, I would like to thank the talented Alex and Emma for effortlessly capturing all of the images in this book, which reflects the warm and rustic style we were aiming for. A special thanks to Lucio and Fiamma for letting us shoot the pictures in their workshop of dreams along with prosecco and pasta for lunch, served in true Italian style. Thanks to Caroline, Woody and Dilly. Thanks also to Tyler Hardwoods.

My star of an agent, Heather Winstanley, who has helped to turn this book from a conversation into reality. Thank you for going above and beyond, encouraging me to take a leap into the world of writing and for your hard work from setting up initial meetings to driving hours to location shoots whilst heavily pregnant.

Last but not least, thank you to the three ladies in my life. Firstly, my mum Dawn who has been my number one supporter for as long as I can remember. Most importantly, my wife Polly and daughter Lilia for your endless support throughout my career and this book, which means the world to me.

3

BBC Books, an imprint of Ebury Publishing
One Embassy Gardens, 8 Viaduct Gdns,
Nine Elms, London SW11 7BW

BBC Books is part of the Penguin Random House group of companies whose
addresses can be found at global.penguinrandomhouse.com

First published by BBC Books in 2024
www.penguin.co.uk

A CIP catalogue record for this book is available from the British Library

ISBN 9781785948633

Printed and bound in Germany by Mohn Media Mohndruck GmbH

The authorised representative in the EEA is Penguin Random House Ireland,
Morrison Chambers, 32 Nassau Street, Dublin D02 YH68.

Commissioner: Albert DePetrillo
Editor: Phoebe Lindsley
Editorial Assistant: Céline Nyssens
Production: Antony Heller
Design & Photography: Smith & Gilmour